A Light to Do
Shellwork By

A Light to Do Shellwork By

POEMS

GEORGIANA VALOYCE-SANCHEZ

Scarlet Tanager
BOOKS
Oakland, California

*Cover & author photographs by Sergio Valenzuela
muwicnatives@gmail.com*

*Cover & interior book design by Fred Dodsworth
fredddodsworth@gmail.com*

Published by Scarlet Tanager Books
P.O. Box 20906
Oakland, CA 94620
www.scarlettanager.com

ISBN 978-1-7345313-5-0
Library of Congress Control Number: 2022933646

Dedicated to the heart and soul of our family:

My father, Joseph John Moreno,
June 5, 1897–August 15, 1991

and

My mother, Rosita Olea Moreno,
November 29, 1917–October 29, 2012

CONTENTS

FOREWORD

Elders are precious to Indigenous peoples as carriers of truth. In a time of propaganda and deliberate "fake news," the truth of a people's history becomes increasingly essential. Indigenous people have always understood how his/stories are needed to continue traditions. During the years when tens of thousands of Indigenous children were forced to attend boarding schools in the nineteenth and twentieth centuries, powwow songs encoded history from the Indigenous perspective. This encryption evaded the mainstream society and its censorship. Georgiana Valoyce-Sanchez publishes with Scarlet Tanager Books a contemporary and equally essential testament to her personal, family, and community history in *A Light to Do Shellwork By*. The poems are songs and histories at once, and they encode a durable culture.

The opening prose poem "The Gathering" sets the themes for the collection: "The old man had been tending the Sacred Fire since before dawn, each branch and limb of oak an added prayer. The rising sun etched the hills of Gaviota in gold, and oak trees cast long shadows from the secret groves where families camped" (p. 1). This morning scene of coffee and sunrise is repeated across the continent wherever Indigenous peoples come together to renew spiritual and community bonds. Valoyce-Sanchez follows this timeless moment with a shift to a poem that is a portrait of an elder, "Chumash Man," as the federal government terminates his tribal standing:

> It's official
> U.S. rubber-stamped official
> *Chumash: Terminated*
> a people who died
> they say
> a case for anthropologists (p. 2)

ix

This pivot to contemporary politics begins a subtle and powerful journey into the rich past of her people and their current challenges. The poem continues with a counterargument:

> Ah, but this old one
> this old one whose face is
> ancient prayers come to rest
> this old one knows
> who he is   (p. 2)

Anthropologists and bureaucrats cannot reduce this man or his experience of sea lion hunting to a form stamped "terminated." In precise language the poet explains the grief and absurdity of the Chumash paradox. His identity is not bogus.

A highlight in the collection is a dramatic verse work, "The Red Shawl," which moves about the page and comes to life in typography and rhythms:

> The middle-aged woman takes
> off her red shawl
> and places it around the young woman's shoulders
>
> The old woman takes
> off her red shawl
> and places it around the
> middle-aged woman's shoulders
>
> The sacred bundle is passed slowly
> from hand to hand   returning
>
> to the old woman
>
> The young woman rises from the circle
> and walks to center stage   (p. 28)

The poem connects generations, and the bundle that comes down through time is the precious gift of cultural tradition, in all its aspects: songs, languages, dances, stories, spirituality. All of these keep communities together individually and as interconnected Indigenous peoples.

Cultural survival of California Indian People is an ongoing miracle after centuries of invasions. They survived three waves of invaders in historical times. The first was Spain, with soldiers and the Franciscan missionaries they brought with them. This ushered in a devastating time for the California Natives as missions enslaved local people for labor and field work. Next, California Indian Peoples found themselves living on land that had become a territory of the Mexican Republic, with limited status and rights. After the Mexican–American War, California became part of the United States. Under the U.S. government, Native peoples lost all rights to defend themselves in court and were the lowest status of any person. In four months under U.S. rule, more California Indians were killed than all the years when they were subjects of Spain and Mexico.

Of the many egregious losses, appropriation of land was one of the most difficult, as this cut away a land base for California Indian communities. Georgiana Valoyce-Sanchez's ancestors—the Islander and Coastal Chumash people—lost all their land. It is now some of the most expensive real estate in California. "Ethnic cleansing" and "genocide" are terms that in no way summarize the horrors of this progressive war on California's Native peoples.

Especially moving in *A Light to Do Shellwork By* are the poems about the narrator's father, in his nineties, as he finds his way through blindness and memories. The respect for this man's life embodies the respect for all the cultural traditions. His people have survived over five hundred years of contact with settlers from the West and East. Prayers, songs, dances, and poems are among the techniques of survival, for a people, and for the individuals. Gratitude to Georgiana Valoyce-Sanchez for this magnificent gift.

Wanishi,

Denise Low
Healdsburg, California, 2022

THE GATHERING

The old man had been tending the Sacred Fire since before dawn, each branch and limb of oak an added prayer. The rising sun etched the hills of Gaviota in gold, and oak trees cast long shadows from the secret groves where families camped. The fragrance of camp coffee and bacon mingled with the murmurs and coughs of people starting their day. When the sun rose above the hills and sparkled light on the ocean below, a young man, bare to the waist and wearing a deerskin skirt and seagull headdress, raised a conch shell to his lips. His breath blown into the conch released a deep cry that echoed through the hills and acorn groves. When the people came running up the hill, laughing and talking, another conch sounded from the hills and the people entered into silence around the fire, waiting for the song that would give form to the gratitude at the center of their prayer.

CHUMASH MAN

"Shoo-mash," he says
and when he says it
I think of ancient sea lion hunts
and salt spray windswept
across my face
They tell him
his people are dead
"Terminated"

> It's official
> U.S. rubber-stamped official
> *Chumash: Terminated*
> a people who died
> they say
> a case for anthropologists

Ah, but this old one
this old one whose face is
ancient prayers come to rest
this old one knows
who he is

"Shoo-mash," he says
and somewhere sea lions still gather
along the California coast
and salt spray
rises
rainbow mist
above the constant breaking
of the waves

THE DOLPHIN WALKING STICK

He says
sure, you look for your Spirit
symbol   your totem
only it's more a waiting
watching
for its coming

You listen
You listen for the way it
feels   deep inside

Sometimes something comes
that feels   almost
right
the way that swordfish
kept cropping up with
its long nose

but no
and so   you wait
knowing it is getting
closer   knowing
it is coming

And when that dolphin
jumped out of the water
its silver blue sides all shiny
and glistening with rainbows
against the white cloud sky
and the ocean so big
and deep
it went on
forever
I knew it had come

My father rests his hand upon
the dolphin's back
the dolphin's gaze serene
above the rainbow band
wrapped around the walking stick

He leans upon his brother friend
and walks across the room
          As he walks
strings of seashells clack softly
as when ocean waves tumble
rocks and shells and
the gentle clacking song
follows each wave
as it pulls back into
the sea

          The sea

          So long ago
          the Channel Islands   filled
          with Chumash People like
          colonies of sea lions
          along the shore   so many
          people
          it was time for some to
          make the move
          across the ocean to
          the mainland

          Kakunupmawa   the sun
          the Great Mystery
          according to men's ideas
          said   don't worry
          I will make you a bridge
          the rainbow
          will be your bridge   only

don't look down
or you will fall

   Have faith

So, the chosen ones began
the long walk across
the rainbow
they kept their eyes straight
toward where the mainland was
and all around them
was the ocean   sparkling
like a million scattered crystals
so blue-green and singing
lovely and cool
some looked down
and fell
into the
deep
to become
the dolphins
they too
the People

My father turns to look at me

Someone told me that story
long before I ever heard it
    It's those old ones
he says   pointing up to the ceiling
as if it were sky

They sent the dolphin to me

I always loved the sea

FAT OF THE LAND

Walking to public school
beyond the Housing Project compound
I would ponder the "fat
of the land"
What it meant
Why my folks always talked
about it

When there was nothing left to eat
but beans   Steinbeck
would appear at our table
blowing smoke rings with his big
cigar and he'd lean back in our
rickety kitchen chair and talk
about the "fat
of the land"

When I got older with babies and
two cars in my suburban garage
my folks went back home
to Indian land
Reservation   rocks   broken bottle-glass
an old shack in the foothills
of the San Gorgonios
    and I asked them
Is this it   is this
It?

Where's the fat?
and my father would lean back against
a scrawny birch   blow smoke rings
with his clay pipe   and smile

I had to admit
the handful of pale pink strawberries
he had coaxed from the stony ground
were the   sweetest   I had ever
tasted

and there was no denying
the singing that took place
when my mother and father knelt
to pat the earth
beneath the bare peach tree

The White Buffalo Painting

For Vanessa Vallez

Grandfather
born in 1897
going blind
losing his hearing and
sense of touch
dreams at night
of the White Buffalo

During daylight
Grandfather sits outside
in the bright winter sun
and pictures
the White Buffalo
on the bare canvas
before him
staring at the spot
in the foreground
where the White Buffalo will stand
"Majestically," he says

His hand shakes
as he brushes a royal-blue sky
onto the canvas
the memory of a thousand blue skies
etched into his brain

He remembers the times he could
accurately paint the sky on canvas
so that the eye followed the sky
beyond the horizon

Now
he wonders if he has brushed
the blue paint on evenly

sensing that he has somehow
missed some spots

The foreground is a peach-sand color
startling against the royal blue
    and lilac mountains float
just above the sand

Weary
he lays the paintbrush down
and pictures the White Buffalo
in the foreground

        the White Buffalo snorts
        and stamps the ground
        his massive head lifted
        to sniff the wind

The earth beneath the White Buffalo
breathes   in all shades of brown
raw-umber and gold   textured
with rocks and brush and boulders

Behind the White Buffalo
stratus clouds trail slowly
across the horizon
and distant mountains become
all shades of blue and purple
changing colors
as the sun flares low

Oak and Pine and Sycamore
fringe the far mountains
and the valley below shimmers
like a dark emerald sea

A herd of brown-black buffalo

moves slowly toward the valley
and the tall green grass

      The White Buffalo shakes
      his shaggy head and
      paws at the ground
      ready for the run

and Grandfather feels
intimately   the energy
of the White Buffalo
remembering the strength of
his own young body
   as he sits
his white shaggy   head
washed in the light of
the late afternoon sun

Long shadows fall
across the bare painting of sand
mountains and sky
shadows that confuse the eye
and force him back
to a world where he has to
walk with hands outstretched
groping
through shadows
that surround him

He sighs and rises
slowly
the palette of drying paint
a promise
he will never keep
the creaking of the screen door opening
a call to home   and sleep
and the White Buffalo

leading the run
toward distant blue mountains
and tall green grass

I Saw My Father Today

I saw my father today.
He lives just across town
but I'm so busy
and what with one thing
and the other
it's hard sometimes.

    My father's face still holds
    tribal memory: aged oak
    and ancient Acorn Gathering Songs.
    A prayer, really.

It had rained for nine days.
Everything was washed to wilting,
like me after a good cry or cussing.
So, we sat in his backyard
making the most of the sun.

Little birds and paper skittered
across the cracked cement. I
strummed my guitar, singing softly
as he sorted seashells and beads.

My father can't hear so well
so, when I sang, he sang, too,
a different tune—something old.
We sounded real good, you know?
Sort of made up our own song.

THE DREAMING

My 93-year-old father fumbles
beneath the bed
for his hunting rifle
gropes in his blindness
dreaming
he is in the Persian Gulf
needing to protect
my mother
who pleads for him
to wake

We talk him home
home
to the waking dream of his old age
the marrow of his dreams
sucked nearly dry
and pain contorts his face
as he inches across the carpet
with hands outstretched
like a toddler
learning to walk

Awake
he smokes and dreams
of all he needs to do
before he dies
paintings his blind eyes
can see   colors
and textures
in detail   paintings
he promised to
finish   his waking
dream   an anxious tug at
consciousness   shaping

the real
from the dream

Each child comes from the womb
dreaming   like my father
dreaming this life
into the next

    Curled like a fetal child
beneath the blue star-quilt   he tries
to sleep again   afraid
to leave
the waking world
unsure
if he is entering the dream
or leaving it

My mother smooths his hair
and talks to him
talks him to the dreaming place
he came from
telling him the war is over
and she is safe
and how tomorrow they will
sit out by Rainbow Pier
and watch the boats
sail out to sea
and how
    no matter what
everything
will be
all right

WHAT IS NOW

Life
that living continuum
that story of time
of self and others
now
and only now
the living Eternal Now
        at this moment
nothing more
everything
now

Einstein
with his quantum theory
of the universe
guesses
space-time dimensions
are many
and curved

What is past?   What is future?

Mystics know
        The Center is everywhere
What is beyond
is in our midst
from galaxy
to flower
divine

See the old man
my father
with his gruff gentle voice
94 years on this earth

but his eyes
clouded with age
are keen
and see into the heart
see old trails
and mountain ranges
see space colonies

beyond the moon
       the eons
       the story
of all that went
into his making
the darkness   and light
all light
and movement   music
one vast dance
within the womb
of God

I am caught up
in the dance
I carry my father within me
and have passed him on
to my children
and my children's children's
children

It is more than DNA

What is to be
already is
    now
the story alive

within each other
within the womb of God

that is without/within us
transcendent
in the living
    Now
        Forever

THE UNIVERSE WE ARE

There is a pull to the sea
beyond its moon tides
and cool blue water
more because the mind
cannot fathom
its vast
depth
and span
our world so subject
to fences
and small
definitive
places

and   so   much   water
reaching   so   far
and so   far
                down
quickens
the spirit
to sense of mysteries
deep
and far-reaching

Along the shore
the thunder and hush
of each crashing wave
echoes my own blood-pulse
as it ebbs
and flows
through my veins

I breathe the salt air
and each cell of my body

rocks in the sea
of its own primordial past

I walk
bare feet   tingling
at the water's edge

and sea-birds dart
and rise   wheeling
on white wings
against the wide
blue sky

   and just beyond
the bend of sea cliffs
rising from a sheltered cove
   seashells
tumble from the waves
into my waiting hands
the tracings on the seashells
telling stories
as I turn them in the sun
reminding me
of the universe
we are

THE INLAND SEA

The desert was in bloom. Blue verbenas and white desert primrose spread out across the sand dunes that followed the windy highway north of Indio, California. Red flowers, as small as the tip of a newborn's finger, bloomed next to seashells in wind-cleared patches of speckled earth. My mother and I were kneeling, marveling at the flowers and seashells, while my father stood speaking into the wind about the markings on the distant blue mountains that traced the ancient sea and how fish fossils had been found imbedded in rock. Wind whistled through the flowers and sand swirled and rose like sea-mist. My father knelt beside us, cradling the seashells and flowers, and the song of wind on water blew across the desert like a prayer.

THE EYE OF THE FLUTE

Enter the eye

From the north
a ribbon of geese drifts
high above the earth

    far below

beside a weathered wood shack
in the spring-green foothills
of distant blue mountains
an old man sits
polishing stone

    Dogs bark in the distance

Down the hill a brown horse
black mane flying
runs along the reservation road
and three children and their mother
stand beside a fence
watching

    Beyond the fence a rusty tractor
sits fallow in the field
silent as the man beside it
watching the horse
run free

the eye watches   the eye
sees   the image
held
to still-point

Silence

Silence that holds all songs
that holds the breath
to play all songs
to life

hush

listen to the music

The horse is running still
hoofbeats on pavement a drum
black mane flying
free
within the still-point
of the song
    the locus of the poem
the eye of the flute

Three children and their mother
stand beside a fence
their father close by
all watching
the horse running   free

Dogs bark in the distance

An old man holds a polished stone
up to the sun
turning it
to catch the light

High above the earth
a ribbon of geese drifts south
the call of a long journey
echoing
across the endless sky

SAGUARO

Desert deer do not lean against
your spiny trunk
Squirrels do not climb and play
along your spiked arms

The harsh traditions have been met
    the years when rain-clouds passed

and did not stay

You hold your secret fruit up to the sky
your nest-egg pods of
    ripe red luscious fruit
and fine black seeds

THE RED SHAWL
A one-act poem

There are three women on a darkened stage

Center stage
sits an old woman
wrapped in a red shawl

      She is nearly obscured in
      the darkness   her red shawl
      like a glowing ember
      in a desert campfire
      at midnight

A soft light grows around her

      In front of her are small piles of
      herbs, sage and sweetgrass, stones, nuts and berries
         She moves slowly
      a ritual   gathering   the herbs
      sage and sweet grass, stones, nuts and berries
      into   a worn leather pouch

      She lifts the pouch before her
         an offering to a familiar deity
      then cradles the pouch on her lap
      and is still

The light dims

Stage left
      A soft light grows
      revealing   a middle-aged woman
      sitting in a hard-backed chair
      close to the front of the stage

She sits   legs crossed
wearing a smart black suit and
black high heels

The red shawl is folded
       on her lap   she smooths it
       Slowly   over and
            over

At her side is a table   covered
with red cloth
A Mr. Coffee machine   dominates
    a white cup and saucer beside it
    a black remote
    a stack of magazines
    Ladies' Home Journal
    Good Housekeeping
    People
    Life

Facing the woman is a television set
It, too, is draped on top with red cloth

As the light dims
       she reaches for the remote
       and clicks the set on   no sound
       only the eerie glow   that moves
       shadows   across the woman's face

       Her hand rests on the red shawl
       folded across her lap

Snap   a bright light   stage right
spotlights   a young woman
in a red dress worn close to the skin
her hands   reaching
for the sky

Her feet are bare

    She moves   a slow dance
    moving to some silent blues song
    to some silky lover blues
    song   wrapping her in
    its steady rhythm

The young woman stops
hands on her hips
head lifted   toward the light

    The old woman begins to hum   an ancient
    nearly monotone chant   a wordless lullaby

The middle-aged woman   takes off her heels
turns off the television set
puts the red shawl around
her shoulders and walks   slowly
toward   center stage

    The young woman leaves the spotlight
    head bent down   she hesitates
    before reaching for the middle-aged woman's hand
        Together
    they walk toward the old woman
    and sit   beside her

The bright spotlight dims to nothingness
and a soft golden light grows around the women

    The old woman laughs
    a pleasing cackle of delight

        I am alive   she says

And nods her head   up and down
smiling   as if at some
      great joke

She nudges the middle-aged woman's side
and the woman laughs   softly   nodding her head
up and down

They smile at the young woman
      big happy smiles
and the young one   lifts her hands
in the air   and speaks

Okay!

    Okay

The middle-aged woman takes
off her red shawl
and places it around the young woman's shoulders

The old woman takes
off her red shawl
and places it around the
middle-aged woman's shoulders

The sacred bundle is passed slowly
from hand to hand   returning

to the old woman

The young woman rises from the circle
and walks to center stage

The soft light remains with the older women
leaving the young one in shadows

She stands
the red shawl draped over her shoulders
holding each end of the shawl
up and out
as if opening a coat
the shawl like the wings of a butterfly
or bright bird

She dances slowly at first
whirling and dipping   whirling faster
the shawl bright wings
the steady in and out of her
breathing   a song
bare feet dancing the rhythm
of her dream

Behind her the old woman
and middle-aged woman   sit
in the circle of soft light

the twirling red shawl like a
glowing ember
stirred to life

The young woman   stops
before them
bathed in their light
    she turns and faces the audience
her arms stretched up and out
the red shawl
    bright wings
poised for flight
as the light brightens
and matures
around her

MAMA'S WATER STORY

My Papago Pima mama
is round and brown
like a clay water-olla
nourishing
giving us life

Mama would tell us about
the clay water-olla
how it would sit beneath
the shade of the ramada
about the hot desert sun
and how she would dip
the gourd into the
cool water
to drink

Imagine
    she would say
as we gathered around her
long ago
in our poor city kitchen
    imagine

She would fill a large pan
with tap water
and we would dip our bowls
as gourds
into the water
to drink
    and as we savored the water
she hinted at the taste
of wet clay
and told us of the water-soaked
edges of the gourd dipper

and how she loved to bite
into the gourd despite
Gramma's scolding

We drank deeply
tasting the gourd and wet clay
feeling the distant ancient land
beneath our bare feet
feeling the hot sun
and relentless desert beyond
the shade of the ramada
knowing
that water
    was life

In those growing-up years
of strawberry Kool-Aid
and ice-cold Coca-Cola
we learned to love
the taste of
water

ALMOND TREES

Driving down Freeway 60 with Mama
toward the Indian Health Clinic
on the Morongo Reservation
in Banning, California,
Mama leans forward in her seat
and asks   Are we there yet?
    Have we come to the place
where the almond trees
aren't there anymore?

So many almond trees
they covered that whole place
all the way to the foothills

In the springtime the white blossoms
were like snow on the mountains
at sunset

    So many almond trees

There it is   there
it is
she says   pointing
to a thirty-acre scar
of bare earth
seeing
so many almond trees
that aren't there anymore

SHE TRIED

For Mom and Dad

She tried to leave him
but the dogs from the farm
two miles away
blocked the dirt road
and when she got back
she wanted to slap him
for the grin on his face
as he stood there
by the wood stove
with his hands in his pockets
except his grin held
so much delight at her
coming home to him
she allowed herself
to be held
    all night long

RACING TO GALLUP

We were racing to beat the sunset
our dusty blue van
racing across Navajo land
through Hopi country
racing to make it to Tuba City
up through Ganado and down
to Window Rock
heading for Gallup
and a night of rest
at my nephew's house

A conference of the American Indian Science
and Engineering Society
was taking place
the next day in Albuquerque
    a prestigious gathering
at the Hyatt Regency

I planned while Mother
drove past scattered settlements
preparing for the presentation I would
give to educators of my summer
at Caltech
    my grandson Ahni in the back
rocking to rap through earphones

A sign read   Old Oraibi
and I nearly missed seeing
the old pueblo
but the road curved around

and I caught it as the sun flared low
        adobe   stone   mesa
        shadows etched in gold
        timeless
as we raced on toward Gallup
and the gathering dark

THE FOX PAW AND COYOTE BLESSING

You've heard of the Fox Paw
It's supposed to be that French phrase
faux pas
pronounced fo pa
meaning a social blunder
a false step
    but I know
that old fox
is a cousin
to coyote

The morning of my Giveaway
at the Sunrise Ceremony
sprinkling tobacco to the east
of the ceremonial ring
I prayed to my Papago Pima gramma
who died a few years back but is
alive somewhere

Gramma   I said
I'm going to do this thing
in thanksgiving for my friends
and I want to do it right
Gramma make sure
it comes out right

So the time came
for my special dance   my Giveaway
last in line
the sun descending
the ceremonial ring
a ring of brown faces
rainbow-ribboned shirts
feathered bustles and buckskin

        and my special dance was called
my husband at my side
his Tarahumara blood resigned
my Chumash father with his
dolphin walking stick
my Papago Pima mama
shawled in black and turquoise

The family waiting
My friends waiting
The people waiting
        and the drum began
        the Southern drum

Just then
in the hush before the dance
that old fox
placed his paw on my shoulder
and steered me north
to dance around the drum
in the wrong direction

Well
Fox and Coyote
led the dance
hopping and twirling around
like Fancy Dancers
all serious-like as if
the world depended on it
and me
just grinning
as if I didn't know better
all my family and friends
behind me
dancing around the drum
in the wrong direction

Gramma   I said later
Gramma   how could you
let me go in the wrong direction?
What was that
Fox Paw doing there?
And why Coyote?
I've never danced the Northern way
except when Alice Keshic's cousin died
and she is Winnebago from the North

By myself I asked her this

And this is what she told me

Never forget
Coyote helped to form the world
For all his Trickster ways
Coyote helped to form the world
The world was made with Fox Paw
and all the seeming backward things
that make the world go forward

Fox and Coyote
travel to the Four Directions
but no matter where you stand
the Four Directions touch you

Still
though you are touched
by each direction
you are from a people of
the red-brown earth of Picacho
Sacaton and southern Arizona

Remember me

We are a plain and simple people
desert people
Our way is not of Southern Plains
or Northern Plains

By dancing Northern
to the Southern drum
you told the people gathered
you were neither

You danced for O'odham
and Chumash   and all the ones
who have no Powwow
to their name

By dancing right   the wrong way
You remembered who you were
    that is a blessing
If it comes from Fox Paw or Coyote

You remembered who you were

PICTOGRAPHS

There are colorful pictographs on caves hidden in the mountains above Santa Barbara that tell of a people who radiated light and danced to the rhythm of moon and sun, people who brought the stars down to earth in ritual and song to tell stories of time when all living things spoke the same language. Sun symbols in rust, red, white and black designs abound in the cave. Blue dolphins swim on rock, the gray of the rounded rock a part of the dolphin's sleek shiny skin. Gold-brown deer fly across star-studded domed roofs. People walk across rainbows. Now people walk miles and climb impossible inclines to reach the caves. But many caves are caged now and people have to reach through steel bars to touch the timeless air—as if it could be caged—and they try to read the pictographs for some clue, some message, hoping to decipher the language that comes to them only in dreams.

LAMPLIGHT

Evening
My cabin hidden
in the high canyons
of the Dorland Mountain Arts Colony
red tar-paper roof
peeking from the trees and brush
like a small red-breasted bird

Among the oak groves
the Great Horned Owl hoots
the dusk
to darkness
    yellow eyes search for prey
among the shadows

Alone
inside my cabin
4:04 p.m. and the sun
has slipped behind
the mountain

Night

Darkness so deep
the mountain is an abyss
a black hole
swallowing the stars
echoing the well of mystery
within me

Shadows abound

In the dark cabin
the kerosene lamp gives off

a soft golden glow
reflecting my own stranger's face
in the window

I write my poems
encircled by darkness
the glow of the lamplight
my beacon
        Together   we hint
of sunrise

SUMMER 1945

Summer   1945
Rural East L.A.
The hills   a gathering of
golden quail   waiting
uncut fields of hay swaying
in the wind   around
my Japanese schoolhouse
home
          abandoned   they said
the wood-frame schoolhouse
mostly one large room with
open wide windows beneath
a gently curving roof
          simple lines
a Japanese painting in
the morning mist

That summer
we lived in one side
of the schoolhouse
long   lazy days   playing
on the wide front porch
shaded by pepper trees
swaying like weeping willows
and I was too young to
question   where
all the children
had gone

At night
coyotes howled
and far   far   away
the war in the Pacific still raged
and the whole world was screaming

bodies gutted   mutilated
arms and legs and heads
torn   blown apart
    Bombs were dropped on
Japan   people burning   running
from wood-paper houses
survivors wishing they
had died   not knowing
that soon
two new bombs would fall and
people in Japan would lift
their faces
to relatives   falling
in black rain

    and I slept peacefully
safe
under a warm quilt
beside my sisters
the hum of our parents' voices
as warm as the woodstove
Mama cooked on

And the day
the bleating wave of sheep
swept   down the hill
    like a flash flood
rumbling toward the schoolhouse
no matter the black dog
    barking at them
no matter the old man
    in the dusty brown hat
    and stick
    poking them

no matter the shouts
    and running to make them

                swerve   aside
they came
        pouring through the open windows
        through the doorway
        bumping and trampling
        each other in the playroom
        milling and crying
        trying to escape their
        awful confinement
and the wooden walls and floor
of the playroom
shook   with their terrible
confusion
the Japanese schoolhouse moaning
and creaking
like an accompaniment to
a Kabuki tragedy
        and I was afraid
in my safe side of the house
        even as the sheep spilled
over the windows and porch
and out onto the dirt road and
they were only a dust cloud
        rising in the distance

FROM THE FRONT OF THE FOURTH WORLD

According to Hopi prophecies, we are now in the Fourth World:
a world that is Koyanisqatzi, or out of balance. The prophecies
strongly suggest that if we do not learn to respect the earth and
each other, this world will end in a terrible way—perhaps in a
nuclear holocaust.

For Robert Boissiere—in gratitude

The Iraqi soldiers
came up out of the earth
like the First People
came into the First World
born
of bubbling fire
the heat of Creation a
fire-wind funneled
to order
to balance
to song
      and the power of the song
created people of all races
and colors
and every living thing
was related
      even rocks and sand
and the Song of Creation was given
to remind the people
of their relations
but most forgot
and the First World
was destroyed by fire

The Iraqi soldiers
came up out of the earth
brown faces blending with
underground bunkers covered with
desert sand
their army fatigues dusty

from sandstorms and
bombs   blasting
the earth
        and in the distance
oil wells burned bright
black smoke trailing
against the gray sky

Fossil-fuel remnants
from the Second World of
gigantic animals
giant flowers and ferns
        a time when people
became greedy
in a world of plenty
and the ones who remembered
the Song of Creation
were criticized by the ones who forgot
the instructions
        and the Second World was
destroyed by ice
frozen
from pole to pole
the ones who remembered
hidden deep
in the womb
of the earth

The Iraqi soldiers
came up out of the earth
speaking in Arabic
telling about no food and
drinking only scarce rainwater
saying
        no more war
        no more war

like the people of the Third World
who grew to be many
and built big cities and civilizations
and some powerful ones
tried to change the course of
the Song they forgot
and built armies and war
machines to destroy
annihilate others
      and the ones who remembered
the Song of Creation
who wanted no war returned
to the earth deep
in the earth with a reed
to breathe through when
the flood was unleashed
to destroy
the Third World

The Iraqi soldiers
came up out of the earth
thousands
with white flags fluttering
like doves' wings
a red sun behind them
flaring low on the horizon
like a distant atomic detonation

      And in some desolate
circle of desert
      five Iraqis
came up out of the earth
their hands raised in surrender
eyes wide and frightened
cautiously making their way to
one blond U.S. soldier who held
a big black machine gun

the conventional voice of the
Fourth World Order
     and the Iraqi soldiers bowed
and kneeled
one man kissing
the hand holding the gun
while the startled American struggled
to maintain   military order
motioning with the gun
     to move over
     get down
but as he looked into the eyes
of the kneeling Iraqis
he seemed to remember   something
that softened the set of his jaw
     You're all right
     You're all right   he said
and the desert sands
whispered in the wind
a song of remembering

CAHUILLA BIRD SONGS

Shadows waver in the fire's light

The gourd rattles hold a faithful rhythm
hold the old Wanikik men
and their song
hold the time
and the dance
constant
      reminding

Sometimes, children dance, too
warming to the fire
in the dark night
warming to the songs
telling the ancient story
with their dance

      The birds, you see, left home
      They went to a land of
      much food   paradise
      until the freeze came
killing

Survivors told of knowing
now   about home

Down the hill the freeway
snakes through the ancient land
indifferent   mindless
of the bird songs
its fast promise like the
sound of distant water
running beyond
the next dark hill

BENEATH THE SOUTHERN CROSS

Just before dawn
in Rotorua
I step outside of the
Millennium Hotel
to catch a glimpse of
the Southern Cross
and Aotearoa's night sky
    southern constellations
    ancient star trails
that I cannot see
from my own night sky
in Southern California

The low clouds
and mist of Rotorua's
hot springs
obscure the night sky
The hint of sulphur and
the fertile fragrance of ferns
fills the air

Rotorua   Waitara
    Pukekohe   Waitomo
I look for Māori People
everywhere I go
catching a glimpse of
    someone   now and then
whose features are a timeless
genealogy
of a People's history
and maritime culture

Like bright stars hidden
from my view   they exist

their light   has traveled far
   what we cannot see
   remains a true reality

Beneath the Southern Cross
and the ancient star trails that
sang them home
   the Māori live

STARRY NIGHT

> We are the stars which sing
> We sing with our light;
> We are the birds of fire,
> We fly over the sky,
> Our light is our voice;
> We make a road
> For the spirit to pass over
> —Algonquian "Song of the Stars"

It is a profound Picacho night
The red earth hills are black against the star-filled sky
     There is no moon
We walk as shadows through the family camp
Flashlights in hand
Some around the central fire   speak
in hushed tones   laughter   punctuating
the darkness
     most are silent
looking up in awe
at billions of stars   alive
and pulsating light
in the dark night sky

Half-remembered star-stories emerge

Seven sisters change to doves
escaping Orion   who always pursues
and then again   they may be

the Blackfoot ones who fled
their poverty   to become stars
or a great bear tracking across
the endless sky
the Milky Way white Papago beans
a scattered trail left by a boy

to tell the O'odham of his new life
the White Bean Trail reminding

in the dark night
that everything would be
all right

I lie outside the tent
warm in my sleeping bag
cool breeze across my face
looking up into the night sky
        taking in the immensity
of it all   a billion stars pulsating in
my veins   my blood
the Mystery   the Universe
still-point
        and flowing

The Big Dipper has moved   slides

down the sky   toward
where the Colorado River flows
alongside the sleeping camp

Ghosts walk among us   Great-Grampa
long dead   the old Picacho townsite
transparent in starlight

Gramma   Daddy   Mama
        breathing in our midst
the light of stars long dead   alive
and shining this dark night

Coyote cubs yip beyond the dark hills

I want to sleep with my eyes wide open
taking in the sweep of night   billions of stars
I cannot   lose   this   but
        I sleep
dreaming   I live

a bird of fire
singing my light
in a universe of endless stars

Note: The town of Picacho, California, was founded by my great-grandfather, José María Mendívil. He was Akimel O'odham (Pima) and Basque. When he was about eight years old, he became a captive of an Apache raiding party. He was adopted by one of the leaders and raised as an Apache until he was about eighteen years old. He was later captured by the United States Army and became a translator. After my great-grandfather married a Tohono O'odham (Papago) woman, Jesusa, and had a family, he founded Picacho. He named the streets after his daughters: Pilar, Ramona, and Lolita. My maternal grandmother was Pilar. Today, Picacho is often referred to as a ghost town. This poem is for my beloved grandmother, Pilar, my mother, Rosita, and my Mendívil relatives.

STARDUST

5 a.m.
the reservation still
the battles of the night before
the hidden hurts that
rise in dreams
drifting
to some lost and fading place

My mother and father sleep
silhouetted in moonlight
    I pause beside their bedroom door
blessed by their breathing
before stepping outside
into the dark cool quiet

The old dog comes from
under the house and
stands beside me

A silver wash of sky
begins low
beyond the foothills
    It is an ancient glow
I know
again

Holy
The silence
The still-point
between night
and dawn
when moon and stars
still cast soft light
upon the hillside

and rocks and stones
shine
become stars
wedded to earth
in some grand cosmic tying

I stand beside the dog
our blood and bones
a spectral band of
stellar matter held
in the center
of the turning earth
   stardust standing
amidst a field of stones
of stars
our eyes turned toward
the rising sun
the new day

WHEN THE ANCESTORS SPEAK

For Lillian Robles, beloved Acjachemen Elder, leader of the fight to save Puvungna, other Sacred Sites, and our ancestral remains

In that hush just before dawn
when birds stir in their nests
and darkness gives way to light
    the Ancestors speak

    Listen

Can you hear rose petals falling
sage blooming on the hillside
the hum of the distant ocean?

    Walking with Lillian
on the sacred ground of Puvungna
there were times
beneath the tall eucalyptus trees
when she would stop
tilt her head
    and listen
as if to some distant song
    ancient voices
whispering in her ears
drifting in the breeze
    touching her face
    her soul

It is mid-morning in October
I am standing on the bank of an estuary
water flowing to the sea
gray sky above Bolsa Chica wetlands

    In the distance   the walkers make
their way back across the mesa point
returning from their pilgrimage

honoring the Ancestors
    Ancestors whose remains and
mysterious cog stones
speak
of their time beneath the sun

Lillian is leading the walkers
    determined
to make this last pilgrimage
    before she leaves this earth
her white hair shines in the morning sun
and wildflowers bloom
in the field behind her

    I have arrived too late
so much going on in my busy life
but I wave across the water to the walkers
the wind at my back   rustling through the reeds
whispering in my ears
    I will join them for the final stretch
of the pilgrimage

Better late than never   Lillian said

Because when the Ancestors speak
    you have to listen

WARRIOR WOMAN

For Robin Estrada and her mother, Roberta Cameron, Kumeyaay,
dedicated to her people at San Pasqual Indian Reservation

Warrior Woman
walking the beach
pensive
beside you the ocean
blue-gray   vast
shimmering in the sunlight
its far horizon   beyond
what the eye can see

The rhythm of the waves
crashing on shore   sings
of the underlying power of
ocean tides
and the dance between earth
and moon

The taste of salt is in the air

You walk the beach
sensing another reality
a reality
we think we know
bathed in a light
we cannot see
where   everything   everyone
essences God

Warrior Woman
so courageous
fighting to live
to be
with your beloved as long
as you can
to live   aware
of the beauty around you

loving this earth
the blues of sky   water
and distant mountains
    all the shades of green
    of plant life and trees
the browns of earth   rocks
and sand
and always   the rainbow
    the fragrance of fresh flowers

We on earth
are so often like the driftwood you loved
our gray meanderings
trying to make sense of
heartbreak
and loss
praying for Creative Love
to shape us into something beautiful

Warrior Woman
you hold the lamp
that lights our path
reminding us
    There is no darkness so deep
    that God is not deeper still

We trust that light
knowing you are there
praying for us to make it
safely
to that Promise
where   Everything   Everyone
Eternally
Essences   God

A LIGHT TO DO SHELLWORK BY

For my father, Joseph John Moreno,
June 5, 1897–August 15, 1991

One day
     all of life catapulted into one
day   one moment
of sunlight
filtering through a high bedroom window
framed by blue curtains
filtering through the waiting
of the grownups
     sunlight
and the laughter of children outside
warming my father's
dying

My father turns his head to acknowledge the sun

     The light   the light
        he says
           and the light within

     It's a good light to do shellwork by

The ocean sang in my father's hands
abalone pendants shimmered rainbows
from the ears of pretty girls
and shellwork dotted driftwood carvings
     cowrie shells, cone shells, volute shells
     red, black, white, blue, brown, green shells
the life they once held
sacred
old stories etched on
the lifeline of my father's palm

I hold my father's hand
my own shellwork   words
my poet's eye noting the light
        how through the bedroom door
the ears of fresh white corn piled
on the kitchen table
harvest the afternoon sun
        how light shines through a glass of water
touches
my mother's white hair as she leans
to embrace my father
        the hush of twilight
and how the sunset
        like a trail of wild lupines
or the tracings on seashells
tells stories
of our origin
as it lights up the sky
with fire

THERE IS A FIRE

There is a fire   burning
        It is ancient
older than the first burst of stars
exploding the darkness
into universe

The fire formed the earth
and flamed in the campfires
of the Hulmolmoloqiwash
those ancient ones
who knew
how to bring the stars down
to earth
in ritual

and song

and in the centuries that followed
        even with all the forgetting
the fire endured

Once   in the hills above Gaviota
in that silver darkness
just before dawn
I saw a man tending
the fire   in silence
each branch and limb of oak
was a prayer
and the fire
was carefully tended
for four days and four nights
burning   burning
while the people gathered

for strength   and good words
and direction

and the fire held our circle sacred

     I remember
one month before my father died
he dreamed
     He dreamed he was swimming
in darkness
and the sea was as black
and smooth
as obsidian
     He was getting awfully tired
  of swimming   he said
     didn't know if he would make it

until he saw the light of the fires
along a distant shore
each fire
a beacon   telling of one
who made it

     It gave him hope   he said
  made him think that he
  could make it   after all

I am sure   I have seen
that same light in the eyes
of the Seekers
who dare to believe
and follow
their own good destiny
despite all of the odds

against them
        I have warmed my soul
in their flame

and I know

that fire   that light
        cannot die

It is more ancient and sacred
than the universe
It will always flare forth
like sunrise
        bringing life
to our sleeping world

ACKNOWLEDGMENTS

First, I want to acknowledge all the writers who helped to give me a voice and make some sense of the rapidly changing world in my young life. My mother and father, who had very little formal schooling, made sure that we had books in whatever house we happened to be living in. Of course, my father loved Steinbeck's books, especially *The Grapes of Wrath*, *Of Mice and Men*, and *Cannery Row*. We read these over and over. My sisters, Patricia and Susan, and our younger brother, John, knew that books were essential. My parents told us we could travel the world and meet the most amazing people by reading books and, most importantly, by listening to our family stories and cultural histories, including the stories of Earth and Water, Plants and Animals. Later, when I went to California State University, Long Beach, in the 1970s, I was introduced to American Indian writers and my life changed forever. I wish I could list all the writers—so many no longer with us—who taught me that I could write about my life as a Chumash and O'odham woman and that my story was meaningful and needed to be told. Later, I taught American Indian Literature, Native American Women's Literature, American Indian Histories and Philosophies, and other classes that I designed; I was the teacher and student at the same time. I taught at CSULB for almost three decades. I must acknowledge Dr. Maulana Karenga, the creator of Kwanzaa, and his wife, Tiamoyo, for their unwavering support and mentorship. The directors of American Indian Studies were many during my tenure: C. B. Clark, Richard Band, Richard Glazer Danay, Mary Ann Jacobs, Lester Brown, Troy Johnson, and Craig Stone. I am forever grateful to Rick Danay for opening the door to my long teaching career. I am grateful to the countless students who were also my teachers and blessed my life. They number in the hundreds. Thousands? You know who you are. I must also acknowledge writer Lucille Lang Day, publisher of Scarlet Tanager Books, who accepted my manuscript, believed in me, and has been my kind and wise advisor throughout; Dave Holt, who saw the light in my poems; Denise Low, who is my new forever friend; Deborah A. Miranda and Linda Hogan, who are my beloved sister-friends, role models, and mentors, always encouraging me to get my work out; and always Joy Harjo, whose wisdom, loving heart, kindness, and awe-inspiring writings will forever bless my life.

Most importantly, I acknowledge Freddie Sanchez, my husband of 63 years, who is my soulmate, the love of my life, and the father of our beloved children, Deborah, Freddie Jr., Michael, Cynthia, and Charles—each so talented and respected in their own spheres of influence. Without them, and our beautiful grandchildren and great-grandchildren, our world would be less wondrous.

I also wish to thank the editors of the following publications, in which some of the poems in this collection have appeared:

Anthologie de la poésie amérindienne (Le Temps des Cerises) "(Écrit du) front du quatrième monde," a French translation of "From the Front of the Fourth World"

News from Native California, Vol. 15, No. 3: "When the Ancestors Speak"

News from Native California, Vol. 20, No. 4: "Summer 1945"

Over This Soil: An Anthology of World Farm Poems (University of Iowa Press): "The Fat of the Land"

Red Indian Road West: Native American Poetry from California (Scarlet Tanager Books): "A Light to Do Shellwork By" and "Chumash Man"

Returning the Gift: Poetry and Prose from the First North American Native Writer's Festival (University of Arizona Press): "From the Front of the Fourth World," "The Dolphin Walking Stick," and "The Fox Paw and Coyote Blessing"

The Sound of Rattles and Clappers: A Collection of New California Indian Writing (University of Arizona Press): "A Light to Do Shellwork By," "Cahuilla Bird Songs," "Chumash Man," "Fat of the Land," "I Saw My Father Today," "Mama's Water Story," "Summer 1945," "The Dolphin Walking Stick," "The Dreaming," "The Eye of the Flute," and "Petroglyphs," which appears as "Pictographs" in this collection

Spring Salmon, Hurry to Me! The Seasons of Native California (Heyday Books): "Summer 1945" and "The Eye of the Flute"

When the Light of the World Was Subdued, Our Songs Came Through: A Norton Anthology of Native Nations Poetry (W.W. Norton & Company): "The Dolphin Walking Stick"

ABOUT THE AUTHOR

Georgiana Valoyce-Sanchez is a descendant of Islander and Coastal Chumash Peoples from her father's lineage, and O'odham (Akimel and Tohono) from her mother's lineage. She is currently an enrolled member of The Coastal Band of the Chumash Nation and chair of the Chumash Women's Elders Council for the Wishtoyo Foundation. She taught many different classes for the American Indian Studies Program at California State University, Long Beach, including two classes she designed: "World Genocides: An American Indian Perspective," with graduate student Anna Nazarian-Peters, and "Conduits of California Indian Cultures: Art, Music, Dance and Storytelling." She retired from CSULB in 2014, after twenty-seven years. She was a board member for many years at the California Indian Storytelling Association, and she continues to be an advocate for California Indian languages and sacred sites. Her poem "I Saw My Father Today" is on display at the Embarcadero Muni/BART station as one of twelve poems cast in bronze and placed prominently in San Francisco.

ALSO FROM SCARLET TANAGER BOOKS

Bone Strings by Anne Coray
poetry, 80 pages

Fire and Rain: Ecopoetry of California
edited by Lucille Lang Day and Ruth Nolan
poetry, 462 pages

Poetry & Science: Writing Our Way To Discovery
edited by Lucille Lang Day
poetry and essays, 72 pages

The Rainbow Zoo by Lucille Lang Day
illustrated by Gina Aoay Orosco
children's book, 26 pages

Wild One by Lucille Lang Day
poetry, 100 pages

The "Fallen Western Star" Wars: A Debate About Literary California
edited by Jack Foley
essays, 88 pages

Catching the Bullet and Other Stories by Daniel Hawkes
fiction, 64 pages

Luck by Marc Elihu Hofstadter
poetry, 104 pages

Visions: Paintings Seen Through the Optic of Poetry
by Marc Elihu Hofstadter
poetry, 72 pages

Embrace by Risa Kaparo
poetry, 70 pages

Catch and Other Poems by Richard Michael Levine
poetry, 82 pages

crimes of the dreamer by Naomi Ruth Lowinsky
poetry, 82 pages

red clay is talking by Naomi Ruth Lowinsky
poetry, 142 pages

The Number Before Infinity by Zack Rogow
poetry, 72 pages

Red Indian Road West: Native American Poetry from California
edited by Kurt Schweigman and Lucille Lang Day
poetry, 110 pages

The Book of Geezer by John Teton
fiction, 268 pages

Call Home by Judy Wells
poetry, 92 pages

Everything Irish by Judy Wells
poetry, 112 pages

*Turning a Train of Thought Upside Down:
An Anthology of Women's Poetry*
edited by Andrena Zawinksi
poetry, 100 pages

Scarlet Tanager
BOOKS

CPSIA information can be obtained
at www.ICGtesting.com
Printed in the USA
JSHW020041060423
39968JS00002B/13

9 781734 531350